RAPID WE

LOSS FOR

BEGINNERS

The New Complete Cookbook and
Diet Guide.Meal Prep Magazine
Program for Quick Weight Point
System.Slow Cooker Recipes.

Furthermore, the transmission, duplication, or reproduction of any of the following work including specific information will be considered an illegal act irrespective of if it is done electronically or in print. This extends to creating a secondary or tertiary copy of the work or a recorded copy and is only allowed with the express written consent from the Publisher. All additional right reserved.

The information in the following pages is broadly considered a truthful and accurate account of facts and as such, any inattention, use, or misuse of the information in question by the reader will render any resulting actions solely under their purview. There are no scenarios in which the publisher or the original author of this work can be in any fashion deemed liable for any hardship or damages that may befall them after undertaking information described herein.

Additionally, the information in the following pages is intended only for informational purposes and should thus be thought of as universal. As befitting its nature, it is presented without assurance regarding its prolonged validity or interim quality. Trademarks that are mentioned are done without written consent and can in no way be considered an endorsement from the trademark holder.

Table of Contents

The information in the following pages is broadly considered a truthful and accurate account of facts and as such, any inattention, use, or misuse of the information in question by the reader will render any resulting actions solely under their purview. There are no scenarios in which the publisher or the original author of this work can be in any fashion deemed liable for any hardship or damages that may befall them after undertaking information described herein.

Additionally, the information in the following pages is intended only for informational purposes and should thus be thought of as universal. As befitting its nature, it is presented without assurance regarding its prolonged validity or interim quality. Trademarks that are mentioned are done without written consent and can in no way be considered an endorsement from the trademark holder.

INTRODUCTION

Rapid weight loss is a well-known diet that assists individuals with shedding pounds through its point-checking framework. You're required to follow your nourishment admission (as every nourishment has a doled-out point worth) and remain inside your day by day focuses spending plan. Since unhealthy or void calorie nourishments utilize more focuses, constraining those will decrease your general vitality admission and assist you with shedding pounds.

This doesn't mean the arrangement is the correct decision for everybody, however. While Rapid weight loss has its positive characteristics, it additionally may prompt unfortunate dieting propensities. A few people feel the steady following is disagreeable, and others may control focuses, (for example, skipping dinners to bank focuses for less solid nourishments). It likewise can be exorbitant after some time.

Adjusted and Flexible

Rapid weight loss offers one of the most adaptable business diets available. By relegating vegetables, natural products, and lean proteins an estimation of zero points, the diet urges you to make these the heft of your suppers while as yet taking into consideration sufficient grains and dairy inside your day by day Points assignment.

Shows Lifelong Skills

Regardless of what diet plan you pick, you need it to be something you can pursue forever. Rapid weight loss shows basic good dieting abilities that will work well for you after some time - like estimating your segments and serving sizes and urging you to cook nourishment at home.

No Foods are Forbidden

There is no rundown of nourishments to stay away from on Rapid weight loss like you'll discover on different diets. Rather, you'll tally Points and gain Points. The point framework urges you to eat well nourishment yet in addition enables you to enjoy with sweet treats or snacks every so often.

Gradual Weight Loss

You can hope to lose one to two pounds every week on Rapid weight loss. A few studies have bolstered these cases and demonstrated the program to be viable for weight misfortune.

For instance, one investigation distributed in 2017 in Lancet thought about weight misfortune among those utilizing self-improvement materials, Rapid weight loss for 12 weeks, or Rapid weight loss for 52 weeks. The 52-week program prompted preferable outcomes over the 12-week program, and the 12-week program would be advised to results than the independently directed program.

Another 2015 efficient survey in Annals of inner drug analyzed a few business weight misfortune programs. The examination found that those on Rapid weight loss lost 2.6 percent more weight contrasted with control groups.

Strangely, a far reaching influence may likewise exist for companions of those taking an interest in Rapid weight loss (or other weight misfortune programs). A study distributed in 2018 in Obesity discovered significant weight misfortune among life partners of those taking an interest in Rapid weight loss, despite the fact that they themselves didn't join.

Huge amounts of Support and Resources

Rapid weight loss offers a greater number of assets than most other diet programs. You'll discover the application and site convenient for figuring and following Points, just as discovering formula thoughts.

If you like responsibility and gathering support, you can likewise go to the ordinary gathering gatherings. You can even pursue a superior participation that incorporates customized instructing for one-on-one help.

Additionally, if you possess a Fitbit for weight misfortune, or utilize another gadget or weight misfortune application like Jawbone, Withings, Misfit, Garmin Vivofit, Apple Health, or Map-My-Run, you can synchronize your action to Rapid weight loss. This encourages you deal with all your physical movement and weight misfortune information in one spot.

Diminishes Diabetes Risk

Because Rapid weight loss steers clients towards nutritious choices and assists individuals with getting in shape, the program has been related with a decreased danger of type 2 diabetes or better glucose control among those with diabetes.

For instance, an examination distributed in 2017 in BMJ open diabetes inquire about and care took a gander at the impacts of alluding those with pre-diabetes to a free Rapid weight loss program. The individuals who took part shed pounds and diminished hemoglobin A1c levels (a proportion of glucose control). Truth be told, 38 percent of patients came back to totally typical blood glucose metrics.

Different studies have discovered comparative outcomes among those with pre-diabetes, incorporating a study distributed in BMJ Open Diabetes Research and Care in 2017. Another study distributed in 2016 in Obesity (Silver Springs) has likewise indicated the individuals who as of now have diabetes experienced weight misfortune and better glucose control when following the Rapid weight loss program.

Advances Exercise

The Rapid weight loss framework energizes a lot of day by day development and exercise. You procure Points with development that assist you with offsetting your nourishment admission. Direction is accommodated new exercisers and for the individuals who can work out more enthusiastically and consume more calories.

Despite the fact that there are numerous advantages to Rapid weight loss, that doesn't mean it's an ideal choice for everybody. Think about the downsides before putting resources into the arrangement.

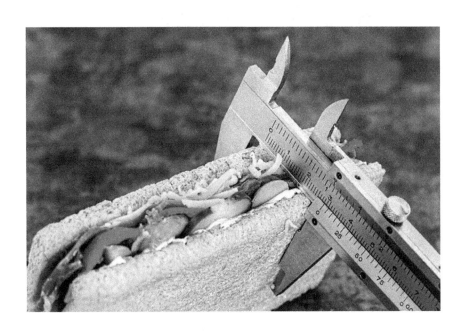

WHAT TO KNOW BEFORE STARTING A RAPID WEIGHT LOSSPROGRAM

When it comes to weight reduction, most specialists concur a solid eating routine is more powerful than work out. Individuals often work out to an ever-increasing extent, urgently trusting they can eat anything they desire. Yet, it's a decent diet that has the genuine effect with your waistline.

That is the reason individuals who effectively get thinner — and keep it off — receive lifelong, smart dieting propensities.

"I wish I hadn't attempted every one of the contrivances and burned through a great many dollars on prevailing fashion counts calories that never worked," Heather Crockett Oram told TODAY, by means of email. Oram shed 82 pounds by changing her eating and exercise propensities. "I wish somebody would have revealed to me it is anything but a win or bust kind of thing."

Oram and nine other ladies share what they wished they knew before changing their weight control plans.

1. It's OK to fall flat.

When individuals initially receive smart dieting propensities, they here and there figure they can never eat a cut of cake or a bit of pizza. Then when they do, they feel like disappointments. Be that as it may, individuals who succeed realize one mix-up isn't the apocalypse.

"The occasions when … my treat day transformed into a treat month, I wish I had somebody to reveal to me that it is OK and simply refocus," Patricia Wilson told TODAY. Wilson shed 100 pounds.

"It is OK to fizzle," she said by means of email. "For whatever length of time that you flop forward — don't surrender, continue pushing through."

2. Eating well sets aside cash.

LeAnne Manuel thought purchasing solid foods cost more cash. That was one of her reasons to eat prepared and low quality nourishments. In any case, not long after subsequent to changing her dietary patterns, she learned she was sparing dollars.

"We really spend much less at this point. For one, the measure of ingredients has curtailed. I eat about a large portion of the volume that I used to eat," said Manuel, who shed 165 pounds.

3. Rolling out little improvements has a major sway.

In the past when Jenna Winchester had a go at getting more fit, she cut every single terrible food from her eating regimen without a moment's delay. This made weight reduction testing because she longed for such a large number of undesirable foods simultaneously and felt overpowered.

Be that as it may, when she began her ongoing effective weight reduction venture, which prompted a 210-pound misfortune, she did it with little changes.

"Begin little. Try not to go insane and cut out each and every awful food at the same time. Begin by removing a certain something, similar to pop or desserts, and afterward gradually add on to that," Winchester said.

4. You feel the progressions right away.

Subsequent to practicing with a coach for a month and shedding 17 pounds, Lydia Dziubanek chose to present lean protein, foods grown from the ground into her eating regimen. She started getting in shape snappier, however she likewise was stunned by how she felt.

"Changing my eating regimen brought numerous shocks, however most significant was the acknowledgment of how much better I felt once introductory migraines left from my body breaking free of the sugar yearnings. I felt lighter and increasingly lively," she told TODAY

5. Sound diets incorporate including not simply subtracting.

When Jordan Kohanim once thought of diets, she thought she needed to limit what she ate. During her 70-pound weight reduction, she understood she could include foods and still get more fit.

"I included more foods grown from the ground," she said. "Cause yourself to eat two cups of veggies before you eat that sandwich."

When she included increasingly nutritious foods, she discovered her longings for unfortunate foods vanished.

6. Food is fuel.

When Amy-Jo Reid originally began getting thinner, she figured she could just have protein shakes or chicken bosom. Yet, then somebody offered her some guidance and eating turned out to be additionally energizing — and satisfying.

"Somebody instructed me to begin taking a gander at food as 'fuel for my body.' That was a gigantic assistance," she said. "Blend it up and attempt new foods. You will be astounded."

7. Focus on enthusiastic changes.

In the same way as other individuals, Dziubanek ate when her mind-sets shifted. It took some time for her to understand that she utilized food to alleviate her feelings.

"Concentrate on changing your dietary patterns when you get focused, furious, or praising," she said. "We as a whole battle with food."

8. Sound food is really delectable.

Following quite a while of noshing on greasy and sugary foods, Brittany Horton figured changing her eating routine would mean she could just eat tasteless, exhausting foods over and over. However, Horton, who shed 208 pounds, learned she wasn't right.

"Sound food really tasted great," she said. "I altogether appreciate the assortment, all things considered,

"I began on a 1,500-calorie diet and it was amazing what you could really expend as opposed to eating low quality nourishment," she said.

9. Segment size issues.

When Manuel began seeing her part measures, she understood she was eating a few times what she ought to be. Estimating her dinners helped her shed pounds.

"There is no speculating with segment size, so purchase a food scale to assist you with arriving at your objectives," she said. "Indeed, even now, about three years into my adventure, my speculations are off when it comes to segment size."

10. Be inventive!

Like Reid, Young immediately became exhausted with eating something very similar for each dinner. That is when she understood she expected to grow her go-to plans.

"Ensure that you have an assortment of plans because eating something very similar arranged a similar way can get exhausting," she said. "Pinterest works for me."

11. It is anything but an eating routine

"Diets are intended to end and significantly after you lose the weight, your adventure never stops," said Reid. "The battle never stops."

Where do I start if I need to get thinner?" I think I have heard this inquiry multiple times over my most recent 10 years in the wellness business. While everybody's outline for weight reduction will (and should) be different, there are unquestionably sure beginning obstructs that work for totally everybody.

You're not the only one if you don't have the foggiest idea where to begin. There are huge amounts of individuals simply like you and you ought not feel embarrassed or humiliated to pose this inquiry. Be that as it may, ideally this posting will respond to this inquiry and you won't have to pose to it any longer – that is my objective!

1. Choose!

This is the #1 most significant thing ever. YOU need to conclude that you're tired of the manner in which you've been living and it's the ideal opportunity for a change. YOU need to hit that point – nobody will have the option to constrain you to do it. YOU need to place in the work each day, so this dedication and choice need to originate from YOU!

I've worked with individuals before who hadn't completely chosen however enlisted me as a mentor at any rate. It was extremely evident because the drive, assurance and any flash were gone rapidly. Truth be told, many even misled me about what they were eating or would conceal it from me when I would go into the room! Gee... .this is for YOU (not me!). It totally must be for YOU!

2. Take A WALK

Strolling has unbelievable advantages and you can do it whenever, anyplace.

Strolling is a low-stress, low-sway type of activity (in contrast to running and hopping) and is an amazing fat killer. Simply ribbon up your strolling shoes, running shoes, preparing shoes (whatever!) and go! This is the ideal time to tune in to persuasive digital recordings, your preferred playlist or a book recording.

Try not to think, simply walk!

3. Make A VISION BOARD

Experience a lot of magazines and cut out photos of your fantasy life, body, outlook, house, and so forth. Put everything on a plug or publication barricade and balance it in a spot that you'll see each day. See it, imagine what it feels like to arrive at those objectives (truly, you can close your eyes) and DECIDE that you will arrive regardless.

I have a great deal of pictures of Oprah Winfrey and Jillian Michaels on my vision board. Also, I often contact their heart and afterward contact mine – as though to move the core of these individuals who rouse me to myself. I couldn't care less if that sounds bizarre, I do that and it's stunning!

4. Try not to DRINK YOUR CALORIES – WATER ONLY!

No juices, no pop, no games drinks... simply water!

Goodness and no eating regimen pop. The artificial sugars still enact the "compensate pathways" that are initiated when we eat sweet foods. In any case, there are no calories in them so there is nothing to kill that switch – in this manner bringing about increasingly more undesirable food desires.

Go for 35-40 ml for each kg of body weight. Also, include 500-1000 ml for each hour of activity.

CHAPTER 1: Rapid Weight Loss with Point Systems

No nourishment is taboo when you pursue this arrangement, which doesn't make you purchase any prepackaged suppers.

Rapid Weight Loss appoints different nourishments a Point esteem. Nutritious nourishments that top you off have less focuses than garbage with void calories. The eating plan factors sugar, fat, and protein into its focuses counts to direct you toward natural products, veggies, and lean protein, and away from stuff that is high in sugar and immersed fat.

You'll have a Point focus on that is set up dependent on your body and objectives. For whatever length of time that you remain inside your everyday target, you can spend those Points anyway you'd like, even on liquor or treat, or spare them to utilize one more day.

However, more beneficial, lower-calorie nourishments cost less focuses. Furthermore, a few things presently have 0 points.

Level of Effort: Medium

Rapid Weight Loss is intended to make it simpler to change your propensities long haul, and it's adaptable enough that you ought to have the option to adjust it to your life. You'll change your eating and lifestyle designs - a considerable lot of which you may have had for quite a long time - and you'll make new ones.

How much exertion it takes relies upon the amount you'll need to change your propensities.

Cooking and shopping: Expect to figure out how to shop, cook solid nourishments, and eat out in manners that help your weight loss objective without holding back on taste or expecting to purchase strange nourishments.

Bundled nourishments or dinners: Not required.

In-person gatherings: Optional.

Exercise: You'll get a customized action objective and access to the program's application that tracks Points. You get acknowledgment for the entirety of your action.

Does It Allow for Dietary Restrictions or Preferences?

Because you pick how you spend your Points, you can at present do Rapid Weight Loss if you're a veggie lover, vegetarian, have different inclinations, or if you have to confine salt or fat.

What Else You Should Know

Cost: Rapid Weight Loss offers three plans: Online just, online with gatherings, or online with one-on-one training through telephone calls and messages. Check the Rapid Weight Loss site for the evaluating for the online-just and online-with gatherings alternatives (you'll have to enter your ZIP code).

Costs and offers may differ.

Backing: Besides the discretionary in-person gatherings (presently called health workshops) and individual instructing, Rapid Weight Loss Program has an application, online network, a magazine, and a site with plans, tips, examples of overcoming adversity, and that's only the tip of the iceberg.

Does It Work?

Rapid Weight Loss is one of the well-looked into weight loss programs accessible. What's more, indeed, it works.

Numerous studies have demonstrated that the arrangement can assist you with getting more fit and keep it off.

For example, an investigation from The American Journal of Medicine demonstrated that individuals doing Rapid Weight Loss lost more weight than those attempting to drop beats without anyone else.

Rapid Weight Loss positioned first both for "Best Weight Loss Diet" and for "Best Commercial Diet Plan" in the 2018 rankings from U.S. News and World Report.

Generally speaking, it's a great, simple to-pursue program.

Is It Good for Certain Conditions?

Rapid Weight Loss is useful for anybody. In any case, its attention on nutritious, low-calorie nourishments makes it extraordinary for individuals with hypertension, elevated cholesterol, diabetes, and even coronary illness.

If you pick any premade dinners, check the names, as some might be high in sodium.

Work with your primary care physician so they can check your advancement, as well. This is particularly significant for individuals with diabetes, as you may need to alter your medication as you get in shape.

If the idea of gauging your nourishment or checking calories make your head turn, this is a perfect program because it takes every necessary step for you. The online instrument allocates a specific number an incentive to every nourishment, even eatery nourishments, to make it simple to remain on track.

If you don't have the foggiest idea about your way around the kitchen, the premade dinners and bites make it simple. They're a speedy and simple approach to control partition sizes and calories.

You don't need to drop any nourishment from your eating routine, yet you should constrain divide sizes to curtail calories.

The accentuation on foods grown from the ground implies the eating routine is high in fiber, which helps keep you full. Also, the program is easy to pursue, making it simpler to adhere to. You can likewise discover Rapid Weight Loss Program premade dinners at your neighborhood market.

A major favorable position of Rapid Weight Loss is their site. They offer exhaustive data on abstaining from excessive food intake, exercise, cooking, and wellness tips, just as online care groups.

Be set up to go through some cash to get the full advantages of the vigorous program. It tends to be somewhat expensive, yet it's well justified, despite all the trouble to harvest the wellbeing advantages of getting more fit and keeping it off.

Part Benefits

Dieters who join Rapid weight loss are known as "individuals."

Individuals can browse a few projects with differing levels of help.

An essential online program incorporates every minute of every day online visit support, just as applications and different instruments. Individuals can pay more for face to face bunch gatherings or one-on-one help from a Rapid weight loss individual mentor.

Individuals additionally get access to an online database of thousands of nourishments and plans, notwithstanding a following application for logging Points.

Also, Rapid weight loss supports physical action by relegating a wellness objective utilizing Points.

Every action can be signed into the Rapid weight loss application until the client arrives at their week after week FitPoint objective.

Exercises like moving, strolling and cleaning would all be able to be tallied towards your Point objective.

Rapid weight loss additionally gives wellness recordings and exercise schedules for their individuals.

Alongside diet and exercise directing, Rapid weight loss sells bundled nourishment like solidified suppers, cereal, chocolates and low-calorie dessert.

Outline

Rapid weight loss doles out guide esteems toward nourishments. Individuals must remain under their assigned day by day nourishment and drink focuses to meet their weight-misfortune objectives.

Would it be able to Help You Lose Weight?

Rapid weight loss utilizes a science-based way to deal with weight misfortune, accentuating the significance of part control, nourishment decisions and moderate, predictable weight misfortune.

Dissimilar to numerous craze diets that guarantee unreasonable outcomes over brief timeframes, Rapid weight loss discloses to individuals that they ought to hope to lose .5 to 2 pounds (.23 to .9 kg) every week. The program features lifestyle modification and advice individuals on the best way to settle on better choices by utilizing the Points framework, which organizes sound nourishments.

Numerous studies have demonstrated that Rapid weight loss can help with weight misfortune.

Truth be told, Rapid weight loss gives a whole page of their site to scientific examinations supporting their program.

One study found that overweight individuals who were advised to get more fit by their PCPs lost twice as a lot of weight on the Rapid weight loss program than the individuals who got standard weight misfortune directing from an essential care proficient.

In spite of the fact that this investigation was subsidized by Rapid weight loss, information gathering and examination were facilitated by a free research group.

Besides, an audit of 39 controlled examinations found that members following the Rapid weight loss program lost 2.6% more weight than members who got different sorts of guiding.

Another controlled investigation in more than 1,200 hefty grown-ups found that members who pursued the Rapid weight loss program for one year lost significantly more weight than the individuals who got self-improvement materials or brief weight-misfortune counsel.

In addition, members following Rapid weight loss for one year were increasingly fruitful at keeping up their weight misfortune more than two years, contrasted with different gatherings.

Rapid weight loss is one of only a handful scarcely any weight-misfortune programs with demonstrated outcomes from randomized controlled preliminaries, which are considered the "best quality level" of therapeutic research.

EVERYTHING YOU NEED TO KNOW ABOUT FREESTYLE POINTS

My mom had done Rapid weight loss when I was growing up, so I was super familiar with the process. When she was feeling unhealthy, she always lamented that she needed "to get back on Rapid weight loss," as if it was the only way she'd feel better.

So, with my mom's ringing endorsement — along with tons of others — I began Rapid weight loss in the summer of 2017. And to my absolute shock, it worked. In about a year, I dropped 60 pounds, 50 of which came off in about nine months.

It hasn't always been easy and, even with my mom to guide me, the program, especially with its changes, can be daunting at first. I wish I had known few things going in, so I'm here to impart this wisdom onto you.

Just a note that everyone's experience will be different — this is just mine. When it comes to weight loss, you have to do what is best for you and what is advised by your doctor.

Get the tools, but don't go overboard.

The awesome and the intimidating thing about Rapid weight loss is you have to figure out what's right for you. Nothing is off limits, and nothing is required. But, it can help to be stocked up with a few key tools before you go in.

A food scale to measure meat, for example, helps you figure out the exact points of your meal, which keeps you from eating too little or too much. Meal prep containers are essential to storing big batches of healthy, homemade treats. Similarly, keeping low-point foods — like PB2 powder, Kodiak Cakes, Western Bagels, Quaker Oatmeal Packets, cans of tuna, beef jerky — on hand helps when you need a quick fix.

That said, you don't need to blow your paycheck on stuff you may not use. Start by replacing some common pantry items with lower-point equivalents. Start fresh, but start slow.

Read up on the more confusing elements.

Like any diet, there can be some things about Rapid weight loss that you may screw up if you don't know better. For instance, fruit is zero points but if you put it in a smoothie, it becomes a point-filled food. Eat one piece of bread during breakfast and one during dinner, and it could be fewer points than if you ate them together.

Some of this will honestly be trial and error, but talking to other members about their experiences and reading up as much as you can is your best defense against rookie mistakes.

Get some support.

I personally don't go to Rapid weight loss meetings because, if "Sex and the City" is to be believed, I'll meet a man, eat half a Krispy Kreme donut with him, and then break his heart because of differences in the bedroom. Actually, I'm mostly just scared of people.

Tons of people find so much joy and support in weekly meetings. If that sounds like you, I urge you to give it a shot. If you're more like me, though, there are lots of online resources that give you the same sense of community.

The "connect" social network on the Rapid weight loss app is a great way to ask any questions you might have and share funny anecdotes and photos during your journey. You can also use Instagram to connect, and even find recipes, tips, and tricks from like-minded people who want you to succeed. (I actually got myself a finstagram just for my weight loss stuff and I'd highly recommend it.)

Something that people don't tell you before you start this program is that weight loss and a healthy lifestyle are amazing, but it can also feel incredibly isolating. Having that support from people who get it is validating. And it will keep you from talking your partner's ear off if they're not on the program with you. Figure out meals you can eat a million times without becoming bored.

I've realized that I can eat one of two different breakfasts every day and not get bored. Mine are oatmeal, fruit, and non-fat Greek yogurt or an English muffin with a hard-boiled egg, Laughing Cow cheese, and hot sauce.

Knowing that I have one meal out of the day figured out frees my brain up to think of lunches and dinners. Plus, knowing I have one meal planned keeps me from reaching for sugary treat when I'm hungry.

When in doubt, simple is best.

People on Rapid weight loss are honestly the MacGyvers of diets. They can find a way to make any kind of comfort food light and plan-friendly, and I've had a blast making lighter banana bread, enchiladas, mac and cheese, and more.

But sometimes, trying these recipes can get overwhelming and, personally, my body doesn't react well to tons of dairy or carbs, whether it's full-fat or not. When in doubt, it's best to keep it simple — lean proteins and veggies are your friends. I always have chicken breasts and some kind of frozen veggie in the freezer because that will likely be lower in points than any kind of concoction I try to cook.

Comparison is the thief of joy.

Remember that community of people I mentioned before? It's a double-edge sword.

My first week on Rapid weight loss, I felt like such a badass. I had been tracking and measuring to a tee and I was so motivated. Then I got on the scale on my weigh-in day and ... nothing. I had been working out and eating well all week for what felt like nothing.

Being on Instagram and seeing everyone dropping four pounds in a week while I had nothing to show for it sucked. I was baffled why I hadn't lost weight right away.

But I quickly realized, thanks to that same community, that everyone's body is different. I would go on to have those four-pound weight loss weeks and I would go on to have weeks where I'd gain two pounds. So did those people I was comparing myself to.

If you sit there and agonize over what other people are losing, you'll get nowhere. Their body is not your body and your progress isn't theirs. What you probably don't see are the weeks that they don't lose either and the nights they go HAM on some queso and chips. Don't worry about how the plan is working for others — focus on you!

Track your "splurge" meals.

The biggest mistake I made when starting Rapid weight loss was giving up on weekends. I would just assume I used all of my "weekly points" on some take out on Friday night and call it a day without tracking it. But because I didn't track it, I would still see those weekly points there, and then feel OK to eat a bagel with brunch on Saturday. And a mimosa. And some bacon.

That's not how it's supposed to work. You should totally feel free to use your weeklies (seriously, use them!), but you should also be tracking everything if you want to be on the program — even if it wipes out all your weeklies and then some. Otherwise, you'll trick yourself into thinking you have more wiggle room than you think.

I am all for taking a few days off for vacations, holidays, or your own wellbeing. But in "normal weeks" track those points, even if it stings.

Try not to sweat the small stuff.

I've spent my fair share of time crying on the scale, despairing out over a meal that ended up being triple the points I planned, or agonizing because the only option at lunch was least 30 points.

Somehow I am still here to tell the tale.

Everything seems incredibly catastrophic and important at the time, but honestly, life sometimes gets in the way of your eating plan. It can feel so upsetting when you know you've worked so hard only to see your progress sabotaged by a rogue cookie craving.

But it's also important to remember that, although we often say life is short, it's also very long. You were put on earth to do more than lose weight and ultimately, that late-night ice cream with your partner may be worth the splurge.

While no one wants to have roadblocks, sometimes life gets in the way. The important thing is not to let a roadblock derail you completely. It's imperative that you accept your lumps and move on ASAP. After all, consistent, slow weight loss and weight management is the way to go. And if you're truly in this for the long haul, you're going to hit some bumps

RAPID WEIGHT LOSS FREESTYLE: FOOD TO EAT

If yearning is your center name and holder tails you like the plague, your diet might be feeling the loss of the Ingredients that convey reasonable vitality and help keep enormous cravings under control. An indication is feeling covetous when your Points Budget is close as far as possible. For a quick fix, start eating the nourishments that can assist you with feeling full more—so you go through your days feeling fulfilled, not starving.

Here are six science-upheld picks to add all the more fortitude to your suppers and tidbits:

1. Cereal

Imminent transient studies propose cereal utilization assists lower with bodying mass list and body weight. Why? One reason is that oats are wealthy in dissolvable fiber, a kind of fiber that becomes thick and gel-like when joined with fluid, says Wendy Bazilian, DrPH, RD, coauthor of Eat Clean, Stay Lean: The Diet and proprietor of Bazilian's Health in San Diego. The oats are thought to affect hunger decreasing hormones which makes it almost certain you'll eat less, and they void out of your stomach at a more slow rate than basic carbs, for example, found in a donut for instance.

Be that as it may, there's one significant proviso: Because dissolvable fiber needs fluid to thicken up, oats appear to be the most filling when they're cooked in water or milk to make cereal. "A biscuit or breakfast bar made with oats most likely won't have a similar degree of impact, since they don't have as a lot of water," Bazilian says.

2. Beans

Prepare them into plate of mixed greens, use them in soup, or puree them into a plunge. Including beans and vegetables like chickpeas, dark beans, and lentils to a dinner expands satiety by a normal of 31%, as indicated by an ongoing scientific audit distributed in the diary Obesity.

When it comes to completion, these little powerhouses appear to pack a one-two punch. They are perplexing sugars, which convey vitality and they are wealthy in fiber. Be that as it may, they likewise have protein, which takes more time to process — which causes you remain fulfilled for more. "It's a moderate, supported arrival of glucose, which can lengthen satiety," Bazilian says.

3. Non-bland vegetables

Veggies like verdant greens, broccoli, cauliflower, asparagus, peppers, and celery have low calorie thickness. That implies that they're low in calories for their serving size—but since they're high in water and fiber, they have more volume which means they occupy more room in your stomach. "If you pick nourishments that have a lower thickness of calories in each chomp, you'll get a greater bit for your calorie needs," says Barbara Rolls, PhD, Director of the Laboratory for the Study of Human Ingestive Behavior at Penn State University and creator of The Ultimate Volumetrics Diet. A valid example: You'd need to eat multiple cups of cooked infant spinach to devour 100 calories, however you'd get a similar measure of calories from only 1 measly tablespoon of margarine. Which one do you think would top you off additional?

4. Eggs

Have them in the first part of the day, and you very well might feel more full throughout the day. One study found that ladies who were overweight detailed that they devoured less nourishment for as long as 36 hours when they had eggs for breakfast, contrasted with when they ate bagels. (Discussion about mind blowing, right?)

That could be because eggs are pressed with protein—which condensations at a more slow rate than starch based nourishments which helps keep you fulfilled longer, says Bazilian. (A huge egg conveys 6g protein.) But that is not all. A little report likewise recommends that eggs could stifle the creation of the craving hormone ghrelin, which could help nix the desire to nosh.

5. Greek yogurt

A cup of Greek yogurt conveys around 22g protein, which will help diminish the craving to eat and keep you feeling full for more. In addition, it's generally high in water, so it includes volume in your stomach. Consolidated, those two things will keep you fulfilled, Bazilian says.

Obviously, not all yogurts are made equivalent. Plain yogurt is a superior decision than the seasoned stuff, since it's free of included sugars which, in abundance, have been connected to expanded chance for sickness.

6. Brothy soup

Beginning with a soup can help check calorie admission at supper time, a few studies appear. Like non-dull vegetables, soups have a low-calorie thickness—all that fluid will help top you off for generally not many calories, Rolls says.

The key is staying with juices or tomato-based soups rather than cream-based ones. Think minestrone or butternut squash. For much all the more backbone—like if you're having soup for a dinner—consider including a wellspring of lean protein like destroyed chicken, Rolls says.

RAPID WEIGHT LOSS DIET: RESTRICTED FOOD

The nourishments you eat can majorly affect your weight.

A few nourishments, similar to full-fat yogurt, coconut oil and eggs, help with weight misfortune.

Different nourishments, particularly prepared and refined items, can make you put on weight.

Here are 11 nourishments to evade when you're attempting to get more fit.

1. French Fries and Potato Chips

Entire potatoes are sound and filling, however french fries and potato chips are definitely not. They are high in calories, and it's anything but difficult to eat an excessive number of them.

In observational investigations, expending French fries and potato chips has been connected to weight gain.

One concentrate even found that potato chips may add to more weight gain per serving than some other nourishment.

In addition, prepared, cooked or singed potatoes may contain malignant growth causing substances called acrylamides. Thusly, it's ideal to eat plain, bubbled potatoes.

2. Sugary Drinks

Sugar-improved drinks, similar to pop, are one of the unhealthiest nourishments on earth.

They are emphatically connected with weight gain and can have grievous wellbeing impacts when devoured in abundance.

Despite the fact that sugary beverages contain a ton of calories, your mind doesn't enroll them like strong nourishment.

Fluid sugar calories don't make you feel full, and you won't eat less nourishment to redress. Rather, you wind up including these calories top of your ordinary admission.

If you are not kidding about getting thinner, consider surrendering sugary beverages totally.

3. White Bread

White bread is profoundly refined and often contains a ton of included sugar.

It is high on the glycemic list and can spike your glucose levels.

One investigation of 9,267 individuals found that eating two cuts (120 grams) of white bread every day was connected to a 40% more serious danger of weight addition and corpulence.

Luckily, there are numerous solid options in contrast to traditional wheat bread. One is Ezekiel bread, which is presumably the most advantageous bread available.

In any case, remember that all wheat breads do contain gluten. Some different choices incorporate oopsie bread, cornbread and almond flour bread.

4. Sweet treats

Sweet treats are very undesirable. They pack a great deal of included sugar, included oils and refined flour into a little bundle.

Sweet treats are high in calories and low in supplements. A normal estimated piece of candy shrouded in chocolate can contain around 200–300 calories, and extra-huge bars may contain much more. Shockingly, you can discover pieces of candy all over. They are even deliberately put in stores in request to entice shoppers into getting them rashly.

If you are longing for a tidbit, eat a bit of organic product or a bunch of nuts.

Outline

Pieces of candy comprise of undesirable Ingredients like sugar, refined flour and included oils. They are high in calories, yet not very filling.

5. Most Fruit Juices

Most organic product juices you find at the general store share next to no practically speaking with entire natural product.

Organic product juices are exceptionally handled and stacked with sugar.

Truth be told, they can contain the same amount of sugar and calories as pop, if not more.

Likewise, natural product squeeze for the most part has no fiber and doesn't require biting.

This implies a glass of squeezed orange won't have indistinguishable consequences for completion from an orange, making it simple to expend enormous amounts in a short measure of time.

Avoid organic product squeeze and eat entire natural product.

6. Baked goods, Cookies and Cakes

Baked goods, cookies and cakes are stuffed with undesirable Ingredients like included sugar and refined flour.

They may likewise contain artificial trans fats, which are unsafe and connected to numerous sicknesses.

Baked goods, cookies and cakes are not fulfilling, and you will probably become hungry rapidly in the wake of eating these fatty, low-supplement nourishments.

If you're desiring something sweet, go after a bit of dull chocolate.

7. A few Types of Alcohol (Especially Beer)

Liquor gives a greater number of calories than carbs and protein, or around 7 calories for every gram.

Be that as it may, the proof for liquor and weight addition isn't clear.

Savoring liquor balance is by all accounts fine and is really connected to diminished weight gain. Overwhelming drinking, then again, is related with expanded weight gain.

The kind of liquor additionally matters. Lager can cause weight gain, however savoring wine control may really be valuable.

8. Frozen yogurt

Frozen yogurt is fantastically tasty, however exceptionally unfortunate. It is high in calories, and most types are stacked with sugar.

A little segment of frozen yogurt is fine once in a while, however the issue is that it's anything but difficult to expend enormous sums in a single sitting.

Consider making your own dessert, utilizing less sugar and more advantageous Ingredients like full-fat yogurt and natural product.

Additionally, serve yourself a little part and put the frozen yogurt away with the goal that you won't wind up eating excessively.

9. Pizza

Pizza is a well-known inexpensive food. In any case, financially made pizzas likewise happen to be undesirable.

They're amazingly high in calories and often contain unfortunate Ingredients like profoundly refined flour and prepared meat.

If you need to appreciate a cut of pizza, take a stab at making one at home utilizing more advantageous Ingredients. Hand crafted pizza sauce is likewise more advantageous, since store assortments can contain heaps of sugar.

Another choice is to search for a pizza place that makes more beneficial pizzas.

10. Unhealthy Coffee Drinks

Espresso contains a few organically dynamic substances, in particular caffeine.

These synthetic concoctions can support your digestion and increment fat consuming, in any event for the time being.

Nonetheless, the negative impacts of including unfortunate Ingredients like artificial cream and sugar exceed these constructive outcomes.

Fatty espresso beverages are quite superior to pop. They're stacked with void calories that can rise to an entire supper.

If you like espresso, it's ideal to adhere to plain, dark espresso when attempting to get in shape. Including a little cream or milk is fine as well. Simply abstain from including sugar, fatty flavors and other undesirable Ingredients.

11. Nourishments High in Added Sugar

Included sugar is most likely the most exceedingly awful thing in the cutting edge diet. Overabundance sums have been connected to the absolute most genuine maladies on the planet today.

Nourishments high in included sugar for the most part give huge amounts of void calories, however are not very filling.

Instances of nourishments that may contain enormous measures of included sugar incorporate sugary breakfast oats, granola bars and low-fat, seasoned yogurt.

You should be particularly cautious when choosing "low-fat" or "sans fat" nourishments, as makers often add loads of sugar to compensate for the flavor that is lost when the fat is evacuated.

CHAPTER 2: BREAKFAST RECIPES

BACON EGG MUFFINS

This can't be rehashed enough occasions, however DO shower or oil your biscuit tin VERY well. I had a preliminary run with these two or three days before I made what you find in the photographs, and I utilized margarine to oil because I will in general abstain from cooking splashes as much as I can. I additionally utilized thick-cut bacon because I had a couple of cuts left. That was not the best decision since it didn't fresh well overall. I additionally had moderate staying issues, however my normal measured biscuit dish are not nonstick. They are those aroused cheapies from the dollar store LOL. I figured out how to get them out yet I tore the bread base a piece. Here's my guineas pigs Trial made with huge eggs and thick-cut bacon—which isn't the best decision

So when I did them "for reals," I separated and utilized shower and I splashed each cup until it was white!!! Had no issue getting them out. I likewise utilized medium eggs because enormous (and anything over) flooded the cup. I likewise utilized a different brand of bacon and normal, not thick cut. You can obviously do this in a Texas–huge size–biscuit skillet, then bigger eggs won't present an issue.

I will alert that you watch these firmly after around 10 minutes since the bacon will begin to get over-fresh rapidly. You need it fresh so the cup holds it's shape however not consumed.

Ingredients

for 4 servings

6 cuts bacon

6 eggs

salt, taste

pepper, taste

¼ cup destroyed cheddar (25 g)

chive, to taste

Uncommon EQUIPMENT

biscuit tin

Planning

Preheat the broiler to 400°F (200°C).

Spot the cuts of bacon in the biscuit tin, enveloping by a circle.

Heat the bacon for 10 minutes.

Expel the bacon from the broiler and spill out any overabundance oil, if wanted. Split 1 egg into every one of the cups, then sprinkle with salt, pepper, and cheddar.

Heat for an additional 10 minutes, or until the egg yolks arrive at your ideal consistency.

Run a knife around the edge of each cup to release and expel. Sprinkle with chives, if wanted.

Appreciate!

BROCCOLI EGG MUFFINS

I LOVE egg biscuits. That is to say, what is superior to having smaller than usual omelets prepared to eat each and every morning? These little folks have broccoli and cheddar in them, but at the same time's stunning that you can blend in whatever you like! I at times use turkey hotdog or chorizo, a blend of veggies (ringer peppers and asparagus, to give some examples) and different cheeses. Whatever I have in my refrigerator, fundamentally. These little folks are Broccoli Cheese Egg Muffins, and they're cracking great.

An incredible method to begin the morning because they are high in protein, taste extraordinary and fulfill me until lunch. You can make these such a significant number of different ways with whatever you have staying nearby in your icebox. Here are some different recommendations.

EGG MUFFIN VARIATIONS:

Green Eggs and Ham – Spinach, hacked scallions, and ham.

Kale – Chopped onion, and hacked crisp infant kale.

Mushrooms and Cheese – cut mushrooms and Swiss cheddar.

Or on the other hand attempt these Loaded Egg Muffins.

I normally prefer to join egg whites with entire eggs, however if you rather use egg whites, that is fine as well. Refrigerate for as long as 5 days. Microwave in 30 seconds interims until warmed through.

What's more, you can utilize milk or plain Greek yogurt, contingent upon what you have and relying upon which surface you like (clue: I LOVE the surface Greek yogurt gives). Furthermore, the Greek yogurt gives additional protein which is a spectacular method to begin the day! The other fun thing about these little angels is they are really a unique formula in my cookbook! It's loaded up with fun, basic and totally luscious plans that are DASH diet-accommodating. Which means they are made with genuine, nutritious ingredients and stacked with herbs, flavors and ingredients that make food taste AMAZING, while at the same time being mindful with how much salt we include.

In this formula for Broccoli Cheese Egg Muffins, I give a scope of how much salt to include, that way you can choose what is directly for you and your needs/needs. I additionally included ingredients like dry mustard, onion powder and garlic powder to give the egg blend so a lot of delightfulness. I am ALWAYS a fanatic of adding flavors and herbs to plans because, well, they're delightful!

How to make Broccoli & Cheese Muffins:

1. Preheat the oven to 180 degrees (375F)

2. Cook the broccoli until tender (boil or steam) and mash with the back of a fork

3. In a bowl mix together the flour, baking powder, cooked broccoli and cheese

4. Add the chopped tomatoes, oil, beaten egg, milk and mix well

5. Spoon the mixture into a greased 12 hole muffin tin (the consistency should be a moist, sticky dough that is quite thick)

6. Bake for around 30 minutes or until golden

7. Transfer to a wire rack to cool.

Once cooled store in an air tight container in the fridge for up to 3 days and eat cold or, if we're at home, I reheat them for 30 seconds in the microwave. You can also freeze them for up to 3 months, just take them out when you need them and reheat once defrosted.

As I make these for babies and toddlers I've omitted any seasoning, so add salt and pepper or paprika, mustard powder or even some fried onion if making them for older children or adults. Alternatively you could swap the broccoli for spinach, leeks, peppers or pretty much any combination of vegetables.

PEANUT BUTTER OATS

Ingredients

1-3/4 cups water

1/8 teaspoon salt

1 cup antiquated oats

2 tablespoons rich nutty spread

2 tablespoons nectar

2 teaspoons ground flaxseed

1/2 to 1 teaspoon ground cinnamon

Cleaved apple, discretionary

Purchase Ingredients

Bearings

In a little pot, heat water and salt to the point of boiling. Mix in oats; cook 5 minutes over medium warmth, mixing sporadically. Move cereal to bowls; mix in nutty spread, nectar, flaxseed, cinnamon and, if wanted, apple. Serve right away.

Nourishment Facts

3/4 cup: 323 calories, 12g fat (2g soaked fat), 0 cholesterol, 226mg sodium, 49g starch (19g sugars, 6g fiber), 11g protein.

BERRY BANANA PANCAKES

Ingredients

1 cup entire wheat flour

1/2 cup universally handy flour

2 tablespoons sugar

2 teaspoons heating powder

1/2 teaspoon salt

1 enormous egg, gently beaten

1-1/4 cups sans fat milk

3 medium ready bananas, pounded

1 teaspoon vanilla separate

1-1/2 cups crisp or solidified blueberries

Maple syrup and cut bananas, discretionary

Headings

In an enormous bowl, join the flours, sugar, heating powder and salt. Join the egg, milk, bananas and vanilla; mix into dry ingredients just until soaked.

Pour player by 1/4 cupfuls onto a hot iron covered with cooking shower; sprinkle with blueberries. Turn when air pockets structure on top; cook until second side is brilliant darker. If wanted, present with syrup and cut bananas.

Stop alternative: Freeze cooled flapjacks between layers of waxed paper in a resealable plastic cooler pack. To utilize, place hotcakes on an ungreased heating sheet, spread with foil, and warm in a preheated 375° stove 6-10 minutes. Or on the other hand, place a heap of three hotcakes on a microwave-safe plate and microwave on high for 1-1/4 to 1-1/2 minutes or until warmed through.

BREAKFAST CASSEROLE

For those of us who don't have solidified destroyed hash tans in our pieces of the world, we have to make our own! See picture underneath for a visual.

Mesh the potatoes first on the biggest side of the grater. Absorb your destroyed potatoes water for 5 minutes, then flush in a fine work sifter (colander) under cool running water until the water runs clear.

Press the entirety of the water out with a tea towel permit to air dry on a preparing plate or heating sheet.

Store in the cooler in ziplock cooler packs until prepared to use in your morning meal!

step by step instructions to make breakfast meal

If you don't have solidified potato hash tans, start setting up that first as referenced previously.

Then, proceed onward with your morning meal!

1. Pick on your ideal meat fillings: frankfurters, bacon, ham or a mix! If including wieners and bacon, I recommend cooking them first before adding them to your egg blend.

For a veggie lover choice, you can forget about the meat.

2. Pick on your veggie fillings: We love utilizing green chime peppers (capsicum) and seeded, ready Roma tomatoes. You can likewise include corn bits, red chime peppers (capsicum), cut mushrooms and diced zucchini.

3. Pick your cheddar: Use your preferred blend OR go with our recommendation of white cheddar with a mozzarella besting.

© theidearoom.net

CHEESE BASIL FRITTATA

The ingredients you'll require

You'll just need a couple of straightforward ingredients to make this delicious formula. The accurate estimations are incorporated into the formula card underneath. Here's a review of what you'll require:

Eggs

Salt and pepper

Crisp basil

Ground parmesan cheddar

Olive oil for the container

Instructions to make basil frittata

It's so natural! Look down to the formula card for the point by point directions. Here are the fundamental steps:

Whisk together the eggs, Greek yogurt, salt, and pepper.

Blend in hacked new basil leaves and ground Parmesan. Prepare for 20-30 minutes (contingent upon your stove) in a 400F broiler. That is it!

The most effective method to serve basil frittata

It's ideal for early lunch – it makes a bubbly, solid early lunch dish. I like to have an informal breakfast spread with this frittata, smoked salmon mousse, banana bread, and almond flour rolls.

It's likewise generally excellent as a meatless supper. When I serve it for supper, I include a basic side dish, for example, steamed broccoli or tomato plate of mixed greens.

TOMATO SALMON MORNING

Ingredients

1 salmon filet (1 inch thick, around 10 ounces)

1/4 cup finely hacked onion

1/4 cup finely hacked green pepper

2 tablespoons spread, isolated

6 eggs

1/4 cup destroyed cheddar

1/4 teaspoon pepper

1 medium tomato, discretionary

1/4 medium green pepper, discretionary

Bearings

Expel the skin and bones from the salmon; cut into 1/2-in. pieces. In a 10-in. skillet, saute the salmon, onion and green pepper in 1 tablespoon margarine. Evacuate and put in a safe spot.

In a little bowl, beat eggs. Dissolve remaining margarine in same skillet over medium warmth; include eggs. As eggs set, lift edges, giving uncooked segment a chance to stream underneath.

When the eggs are set, spoon salmon blend more than one side, then sprinkle with cheddar and pepper; overlap omelet over filling. Spread and let represent 1-1/2 minutes or until the cheddar is liquefied.

If wanted, make a tomato rose. With a little sharp knife, strip the skin in a flimsy nonstop strip, beginning from the base of the tomato. Move up firmly, skin side out, from the stem end. Fold end of strip under rose and spot on omelet. From green pepper, cut two leaves. Organize on each side of tomato rose.

CHAPTER 3: FREESTYLE SOUPS AND STEWS

STEAK BEAN SOUP

This Beef and Bean Soup formula is anything but difficult to get ready. What's more, it just shows signs of improvement the more it sits and holds up until you're prepared to eat up it. Our family has consistently appreciated cooking with beans (Bush's Beans being our top choice). Beans not just loan great flavor and surface to any dish, yet they are thoroughly filling and have numerous dietary advantages as well.

I adjusted Beef and Bean Soup from our preferred Beef and Barley Soup that I have made for around fifteen years now. I chose to supplant the grain with white beans since white beans can include a similar sort of smoothness to dishes like what grain will in general give the Beef and Barley Soup. Furthermore, let me simply state, it was a consummately delicious substitution. So heavenly thus fulfilling. This is without a doubt a healthy soup, ideal for those with a hunger!

Ingredients

2 ribeye steaks

1 teaspoon ground cumin

1 teaspoon garlic powder

1/2 teaspoon dried thyme

1/2 teaspoon salt

1/2 teaspoon dark pepper

1/2 onion slashed

2 15-ounce jars dark beans (I use Bush's)

2 cloves garlic slashed

1 cup hamburger stock

Guidelines

Combine dry Ingredients through dark pepper and rub onto ribeye steaks. Spot steaks into a ziptop pack and spot in the icebox to marinate in any event one hour to medium-term, liked, however should be possible just before cooking.

Warmth skillet or barbecue container over medium warmth. Sprinkle daintily with olive oil. Expel steaks from the ziptop sack and spot into the skillet or on the flame broil dish. Burn on each side for around 3-5 minutes for each side. Put in a safe spot and permit to rest as the soup is cooking.

Add onion to skillet and saute until translucent, around 3 minutes.

Empty dark beans into medium pan over medium heat. Include onion, garlic, and hamburger stock. Cook for around 10 minutes.

Cut steak into flimsy cuts or into reduced down pieces and spot into soup.

Serve warm with harsh cream and destroyed cheddar.

CHICKEN CORN SPINACH SOUP

Ingredients

2-3 tablespoons olive oil (in addition to extra)

1/2 enormous yellow onion, finely cleaved (about a cup)

2 celery ribs, finely cut and slashed (around 3/4 cup)

1 jalapeño pepper, seeded and finely minced

2 tablespoons universally handy flour

1 cup chicken juices (in addition to extra)

2 cups milk (whatever thoughtful you like, I utilized entire milk because that is the thing that I placed in my espresso!)

2 bone-in skin-on chicken bosoms (OR, skirt this progression and simply purchase a rotisserie chicken, shred that up until you have around two cups)

3 ears of new corn pieces (OR (1)one 10-oz pack of solidified sweet corn)

1-14 oz container of cream-style corn (ah-ha! the mystery fixing!)

1/2 teaspoon dried thyme

1/4 teaspoon cayenne pepper

Salt and new ground dark pepper to taste

Discretionary

Daintily cut jalapeño to embellish

Finely hacked parsley to decorate

Slashed Green Chile*

Broil the chicken

Preheat your broiler to 400°. Pat the chicken dry with paper towels and afterward generously season both side with salt and pepper, or any flavoring blend you may like. Spot the chicken on a rimmed preparing sheet (canvassed in foil for simple tidy up) and sprinkle with a touch of olive oil. Spot this into the stove (top rack) for 35 minutes. Expel from the stove and put aside until it is cool enough to deal with. When you can, evacuate the chicken skin and bones, and shred the chicken into reduced down pieces.

While the chicken is simmering

Warmth a few tablespoons of olive oil (enough to cover the base) in a huge soup pot or Dutch stove over medium - medium high warmth. Include onion, celery and jalapeño; mix and cook for around ten minutes, or until delicate. Add a touch of salt to help this along. Include the flour, and mix and cook one more moment. Mix in the milk and stock, and keep cooking and blending until the soup starts to thicken, around 5 minutes. Then include the jar of cream style corn, thyme, cayenne pepper, mix to consolidate. Include the destroyed chicken and pack of solidified corn, and let this cook until the chicken and corn are warmed through. Taste for flavoring, and include an additional sprinkle of stock if the soup appears to be excessively thick.

Present with daintily cut jalapeño to embellish, or only a sprinkle of parsley - or both!

Far superior extra, you can solidify the rest of as long as a month and fulfill yourself after all other options have been exhausted. Shock! Lunch anticipates in your cooler.

TOMATO HERB SOUP

Ingredients

1 Tbs. olive oil

3/4 cup hacked onion

2 cloves garlic, hacked

1 Tbs. hacked new oregano or basil

1 tsp. hacked new thyme or 1/4 tsp. dried

5 cups diced new tomatoes (2 lb.)

1/2 cups low-sodium vegetable soup

2 1/2 Tbs. tomato glue

2 tsp. sugar

Arrangement

In huge pot, heat oil over medium warmth. Include onion, garlic, oregano or basil and thyme and cook, mixing often, until onion starts to soften, around 5 minutes. Include tomatoes and cook, blending infrequently, 5 minutes. Mix in stock, tomato glue and sugar. Season to taste with salt and newly ground pepper.

Heat soup to the point of boiling. Lessen heat; stew, revealed, 15 minutes. Utilizing submersion blender, process until smooth.

Spoon into serving bowls and enhancement with crisp herbs.

POTATO BEAN STEW

Ingredients

For the garlic plunge

6 garlic cloves, stripped

250ml/9fl oz additional virgin olive oil

1 tsp salt

1 tsp sherry vinegar

For the potato and bean stew

2 tbsp olive oil

50g/2oz breadcrumbs

3 red onions, stripped and finely cleaved

4 garlic cloves, cleaved

750g/1lb 10oz potatoes, unpeeled, cut into huge 3D shapes

250ml/9fl oz vegetable stock

4 tomatoes, stripped, cleaved

1 can cannellini beans, depleted

1 bunch new mint leaves

1 tbsp new parsley, cleaved

75g/2½oz spread

½ lemon, squeeze as it were

Step by step instructions to recordings

Technique

Preheat the broiler to 180C/350F/gas 4.

For the garlic plunge, place the garlic into a heating dish and sprinkle over the olive oil. Hurl well to cover, then dish in the broiler for 25 minutes, or until the garlic is delicate and brilliant.

Move the garlic and oil into a food processor, include the salt and sherry vinegar and mix to a smooth purée. Put in a safe spot.

For the potato and bean stew, heat the olive oil in a dish and tenderly fry the breadcrumbs for 3-4 minutes, or until softened. Include the onions and garlic and cook for 8-10 minutes, or until the onions are delicate and translucent.

Add the potatoes and stock to the dish, then decrease the warmth and permit to stew for 10-12 minutes.

Include the tomatoes and beans and stew for another 4-5 minutes, then mix in the herbs, spread and lemon juice.

To serve, spoon the stew into serving bowls. Serve the garlic plunge close by, or spoon over the stew.

CHICKEN MUSHROOM SOUP

Ingredients

2 tablespoons margarine

1 tablespoon olive oil

1 pound boneless chicken bosoms, diced

1/2 cup diced carrot

1 enormous rib celery, diced

12 to 16 ounces cut mushrooms, a blend of new mushroom assortments, if wanted

1 clove garlic, minced

4 green onions, cut

2 tablespoons flour

4 cups chicken juices

1/2 teaspoon dried leaf thyme

1/2 teaspoon salt, or to taste

Crisp ground dark pepper

3/4 cup substantial cream

Technique

In an enormous pot, heat spread and olive oil over medium-low warmth. Include the onion and garlic and mix until delicate however not seared.

Include diced chicken, carrot, and celery; cook, blending, until chicken is about cooked through.

Include the mushrooms and keep cooking, blending, until mushrooms are delicate. Mix in flour until mixed; include chicken soup and thyme.

Bring to a stew, blending. Spread and decrease warmth to low; cook for around 10 to 16 minutes, until vegetables are delicate. Add salt and pepper to taste; mix in cream and warmth through.

TURKEY GREEN BEAN SOUP

Ingredients

2 cloves garlic, squashed and finely cleaved

2 tablespoons olive oil

1 onion, slashed

1 carrot, finely slashed

1 stalk celery, finely slashed

1 tablespoon slashed crisp sage leaves, if wanted

2 containers (32 oz each) Progresso™ chicken juices

1 narrows leaf

2 cups green beans, cut into 1-inch pieces*

1 sweet potato, diced*

1/2 cup uncooked little pasta, for example, orzo or pastina

3 cups diced cooked dim turkey meat

Steps

In an enormous soup pot, heat garlic in the olive oil. Permit to dark colored somewhat and include onion, carrot and celery. Spread; sweat over medium-low heat until softened, 7 or 8 minutes. Add the hacked sage to the soup pot alongside the juices and the sound leaf. Bring to a stew. When stewing, include the green beans, sweet potato and pasta to the soup. Bring it back up to a stew; lower warmth and cook for around 10 minutes or until vegetables are delicate and pasta is cooked. Mix in turkey. Turn the warmth off. Spread, and permit to sit and steam for 5 to 7 minutes.

Master Tips

3 cups remaining cooked Thanksgiving side vegetables can be utilized instead of the new vegetables.

GINGER CARROT SOUP

Ingredients

2 tablespoons sweet cream margarine

2 onions, stripped and slashed

6 cups chicken juices

2 pounds carrots, stripped and cut

2 tablespoons ground crisp ginger

1 cup whipping cream

Salt and white pepper

Harsh cream

Parsley sprigs, for decorate

Bearings

In a 6-quart dish, over medium high warmth, include margarine and onions and cook, mixing often, until onions are limp. Include juices, carrots, and ginger. Spread and heat to the point of boiling. Decrease warmth and stew until carrots are delicate when punctured.

Expel from warmth and move to a blender. Try not to fill the blender the greater part way, do it in clumps if you need to. Spread the blender and afterward hold a kitchen towel over the highest point of the blender*. Be cautious when mixing hot fluids as the blend can spurt out of the blender. Heartbeat the blender to begin it and afterward puree until smooth. Come back to the container and include cream, mix over high warmth until hot. For a smoother flavor heat soup to the point of boiling, include salt and pepper, to taste.

Spoon into bowls and enhancement with spot acrid cream and parsley sprigs.

CHICKEN BRUSSELS SOUP

Much like its cruciferous cousin, cauliflower, Brussels sprouts transform into a superbly rich and velvety soup just by cooking this vegetable with aromatics and spinning it up in a stock. This beef winds up having an a lot further nutty flavor than you may expect, just as a thicker, more fulfilling surface than you would envision that these minor cabbages might contain.

You can include a touch of cream for a considerably creamier impact, however it isn't vital since this beef holds up individually without the additional cream.

This Brussels grows formula is a beautiful first course to an extravagant supper, in the interim, fills in as a delightful base for a vegan supper with a green serving of mixed greens and some generous entire grain bread for a total feast.

Ingredients

1 pound brussels grows

1 rib celery

1 huge shallot or little leek

1 to 2 tablespoons spread

1/2 teaspoon fine ocean salt, in addition to additional to taste

3 cups chicken stock or vegetable juices

Steps to Make It

Accumulate the ingredients.

Trim off and dispose of the stem parts of the bargains grows. Generally slash the sprouts, if they are enormous. The Brussels sprouts will get puréed at last, so while even pieces will cook all the more equally, this isn't a stunner challenge. Regardless of how you have prepared them saved them.

Trim and generally cleave the celery; strip and generally hack the shallot or leek.

Warmth the margarine in a little pot over medium-high warmth. When it is dissolved, include the celery and the shallot. Sprinkle with the salt and cook, mixing regularly, until the vegetables are delicate, around 3 minutes.

Include the cleaved Brussels sprouts and mix to consolidate. Cook, mixing every so often until the Brussels sprouts turn a more brilliant shade of green, around 2 minutes. Include the stock and heat everything just to the point of bulling.

Diminish the warmth to keep up an unfaltering stew, spread somewhat, and cook until the Brussels sprouts are totally delicate around 10 minutes.

Utilize a hand-held submersion blender to totally purée the soup. (You can likewise do this in a blender, however simply make certain to give the soup a chance to cool somewhat first, work in bunches, and put a kitchen towel over the highest point of the blender in the event that the warmth of the soup makes it splatter out.) Be certain to purée the soup somewhat longer than you may might suspect is important; you need the last item to be as smooth as could reasonably be expected.

Mix in cream, if you like.

Serve the soup hot, with an embellishment of crisply ground dark pepper to taste.

Use Caution When Blending Hot Ingredients

Steam grows rapidly in a blender, and can make ingredients splatter all over or cause consumes. To anticipate this, fill the blender only 33% of the route up, vent the top, and spread with a collapsed kitchen towel while mixing.

CPSIA information can be obtained
at www.ICGtesting.com
Printed in the USA
BVHW092021190421
605310BV00004B/331